into **law**

positive experiences of disabled people

Skill
National Bureau
for Students
with Disabilities

LINKLATERS
& ALLIANCE

ALLEN & OVERY

ISBN 1 869965 23 X

Acknowledgments

Skill is grateful to Linklaters & Alliance, Allen & Overy,
Clifford Chance, Lovells and The Law Society for their
financial support of this publication.

Thanks to Janet Copeman and others at Edinburgh
University Careers Service, all those at King's College
London Careers Service, Judith McDermott and the
Group for Solicitors with Disabilities, John Grant,
Les Allamby at the Northern Ireland Law Centre,
Alistair Graham at Thorntons in Scotland, Felicity Kirk
at Clifford Chance, Jamile Ferreira, Sam Fothergill,
all those who wrote profiles and those who helped
find them.

contents

into law

1 Introduction

You have picked up this booklet and started to read. Maybe you are a disabled person considering a career in law. Perhaps you are a legal employer employing a disabled person. Well, this booklet sets out to show **disabled people succeeding as lawyers**, and describes the range of careers available. Whether you fancy performing in court, in Kavanagh QC style, working at the heart of government on the legal implications of national policy or contributing to your local community as a legal advice worker, law caters for such interests and aspirations, and more. **Whatever your preference, it is mental agility and determination that count, not physical prowess.**

These pages contain information to guide your thoughts and plans about a legal career. There is information about alternative career routes (the different qualifications and training paths) and funding. There are personal narratives by disabled 'lawyers' who now reveal all about how they have progressed in their careers, overcoming challenges they faced. Finally, there are details of some useful publications and organisations to contact.

As a disabled person starting a career in law, you are in an exceptional position at this time. We are at the dawn of a new age in disability law, with the arrival of the 'disability in education' bill and the recent establishment of the new Disability Rights Commission. Some of you may choose to use your training to help make the law offer a better deal to disabled people in the future. **We are going to need disabled lawyers to provide the knowledge and insight to help give Britain the disability legislation it needs.**

2 Careers

The variety of legal professions means you need to decide exactly what kind of career in law interests you. There are alternatives to the stereotypical images of bewigged barristers and city-slick lawyers. The time and money the different routes require also vary enormously. Some careers have clear routes of entry while others are less obviously accessible. The legal world can be an intimidating one, full of traditions and specialist language, so be focused about your choices. Below are descriptions of the type of work involved in some of the main legal careers.

Solicitors and barristers/Advocates Solicitors act on instructions from clients, applying the law to the situation as appropriate. They now have a greater role in advocacy, which in the past was the preserve of barristers. They have 'rights of audience' (i.e. they can represent clients in court) in the lower courts and before tribunals. Solicitors can specialise, choosing subjects during their training that will influence their ultimate career.

Numerous large commercial firms dominate the scene in the City of London and also exist across the UK. There are four main areas of practice:

- **company/commercial** (e.g. take-overs, mergers)
- **litigation** (court battles)
- **property** (e.g. conveyancing, development and planning)
- **tax, trusts, probate** (e.g. wills, charities, estates). In these big firms, clients tend to be large 'blue chip' companies, banks and public institutions.

'Niche' firms specialise in single areas such as shipping, the environment or medical negligence. High street practitioners typically do domestic conveyancing, landlord and tenant work, divorces and wills. Many also do government-funded legal aid work. In addition, community legal centres offer free legal advice to the public on a wide range of community issues such as welfare benefits, immigration, juvenile crime, family and housing. Training opportunities are rare at such centres.

In-house solicitors work for non-legal companies to advise in a legal capacity on issues likely to affect the company, including finance, employment, property, contracts, litigation and intellectual property. In-house solicitors may work in almost any setting, including industry, charities or the commercial sector.

Solicitors in local government are likely to be involved in a range of issues that affect the community such as social services, education and strategic planning. They may be called upon to advise councillors and act for them in courts or at planning enquiries and employment tribunals.

Barristers/advocates are specialists with expertise in advocacy and 'rights of audience' in all courts. They are approached by solicitors (and sometimes by surveyors, accountants and patent agents) to present cases and represent clients in court and before tribunals and public enquiries. Barristers/advocates also advise on complex points of law and evidence. There is wide variety in the work they do. Criminal barristers/advocates will regularly appear in court, often with little notice. Chancery barristers however, spend time researching complex problems on trusts and property. They will then submit detailed opinions to solicitors.

Barristers/advocates are mostly self-employed although some are employed by the Crown Prosecution Service (England and Wales) to prosecute on behalf of the state, for example, in criminal cases involving the police. Like solicitors, they may specialise. For example, there are family sets, judicial review sets and the commercial bar.

Government lawyers, who may be solicitors or barristers, work in central government departments, agencies and public bodies. In central government they advise ministers and policy workers on legal implications of policy issues, instruct parliamentary

counsel on primary legislation and draft secondary
legislation. They ensure that new legislation does not
infringe current law or interfere with basic human rights.
Most lawyers join after qualification as a solicitor but in
London, training contracts are available in central
government on completion of the LPC.

Another niche opportunity is that of Clerk to the
Justices in magistrates' courts in England and Wales.
Clerks are solicitors or barristers with at least five years'
experience. Their role is both legal and managerial.
The Clerk must advise magistrates on the law while
magistrates determine guilt or innocence and impose
a sentence. The clerk also runs the court as a whole.
The magistrates/Justices of the Peace are usually
lay-volunteers who undergo basic training in order to
preside at trials in magistrates' courts. Magistrates'
courts resolve proceedings in both criminal and
civil cases.

Other opportunities

Graduate positions Law Commission Research
Assistants (London) The Law Commission makes
recommendations to government for law reform.
It recruits law graduates (or similar) as research
assistants. A strong academic background is
required. Research assistants work with project teams
specialising in a particular legal field. The law is

reviewed and proposals for change put forward.

Paralegals Firms increasingly rely on law graduates to carry out legal support roles. Sometimes paralegals have their own caseload that they manage independently. The work may also be routinely clerical, or similar to that of a trainee solicitor. Paralegals often specialise and they can be particularly important in the litigation field where huge volumes of papers need to be organised for court. Currently there is no widely recognised training or qualification. Paralegals may work in the public sector. They are frequently recruited through agencies.

Outdoor Clerks Legal aid firms may employ graduates with a legal background as outdoor clerks, often on short-term contracts. The role involves delivering messages, attending police stations to take statements and making notes of proceedings in court. Training is on-the-job.

Academia You may wish to use your law degree as a foundation for academic life rather than going into practice. As a postgraduate student and later as a lecturer/professor (etc), you will be able to combine research and writing in an area of law that interests you with the more practical skill of teaching others who share your interest in law.

Non-graduate careers

Clerks Clerks, also called practice managers or chambers' directors, work for barristers, obtaining suitable cases, known as 'briefs', to maintain their workload, and afterwards negotiating and collecting fees. They also arrange court dates with court staff. It is a tiny profession and difficult to enter. Training is on-the-job. Entry qualifications required are basic (for example, GCSE maths and English at grade C in England and Wales). Entrants may have backgrounds in law, teaching or personnel.

Court officials Court officials are responsible for the smooth running of the court service, including organising the court lists (timetable of hearings). The jobs are standard administrative-type office jobs at different levels. Training is on-the-job. Entry at the most basic level requires few qualifications.

Legal executives Legal executives are qualified, legal professionals (under ILEX in England and Wales) who provide support in procedural and legal matters. Like solicitors, they specialise. They are also Commissioners for Oaths and can administer oaths and affidavits. If not based in a solicitor's firm, they may work in industry, commerce or government. ILEX does not exist in Northern Ireland and Scotland.

Legal secretaries Legal secretaries normally work for solicitors or within a legal department of a company. They work on routine legal procedures: typing up legal documents, administration and correspondence.

Distant horizons...

Queen's Counsel (QC) QCs are senior barristers, selected by an archaic and mysterious process guaranteeing much speculation about who will be chosen next. Barristers must apply to the Lord Chancellor's office to become QCs, and it is the view of judges that prevails. Only one in seven applications is successful.

Judges Judges preside over trials at court and pass sentence. In criminal trials they are responsible for directing the jury on matters of law so that the jury can determine matters of fact, including guilt or innocence. There are various different levels of seniority, from district judge in a county court to law lord in the supreme court, the House of Lords. To become a judge you must be a suitably experienced solicitor or barrister/advocate.

3 Qualifications and training

Solicitor (England and Wales)

Qualifying Law Degree A qualifying law degree lets you progress to the Legal Practice Course or Bar Vocational Course depending on whether you wish to become a solicitor or barrister, respectively. It may take the form of a standard undergraduate law degree, lasting three years, or six years part-time. Some institutions will offer variations such as combined degrees in which you study law alongside one or more other subjects but law must make up at least fifty percent of the course. In all cases, you must study the Seven Foundations of Legal Knowledge: contract, tort, equity and trusts, criminal law, land law, constitutional and administrative law, and European Community law.

Postgraduate Diploma in Law (also known as the Common Professional Examination/CPE)
This is a one year conversion course (two years part-time) covering the same seven topics as the qualifying law degree, aimed at non-law graduates who wish to undertake the Legal Practice Course or Bar Vocational Course in order to become solicitors or barristers. A central board handles applications.

Would-be solicitors must apply to the Law Society for a Certificate of Completion of the Academic Stage

three

3

of Training that confirms the award of a qualifying law degree or CPE.

Legal Practice Course (LPC) The Legal Practice Course (LPC) follows the qualifying law degree or CPE as the next stage in training for aspiring solicitors. It lasts one year, or two years part-time, and has a vocational bias. Compulsory subjects, such as business law and litigation, combine with 'electives' of your choice, such as family or media law. The skills-base covers advocacy, legal research, drafting and interviewing/advising clients.

Training contract After completing the Legal Practice Course you need to undertake a two-year training contract before you become a fully qualified solicitor. Typically this will take place at a solicitor's firm. Many firms recruit two years in advance. A training contract is a 'proper' job with a salary, and must provide experience in at least three heads of law including contentious and non-contentious areas.

Professional Skills Course (PSC) During your training contract, you must also undertake the Professional Skills Course before you can qualify as a solicitor. As with the LPC, there are compulsory elements and electives covering areas such as financial skills, advocacy and ethics.

Barrister (England and Wales)

Bar Vocational Course The Bar Vocational Course (BVC) follows either the qualifying law degree or the Postgraduate Diploma in Law as the next stage of vocational training for aspiring barristers. It is a one-year full-time course combining knowledge and skills, including case studies, advocacy, professional attitudes and conduct. It is offered part-time at just one institution, the Inns of Court School of Law in London. On successful completion of the BVC you will be called to the Bar, but you cannot practise as a barrister unless you get a 'pupillage' (traineeship).

Before you can register for the BVC, you must be admitted to one of the four Inns of Court. The Inns are non-academic societies that provide collegiate and educational activities, and support for barristers and student barristers. The Inns alone have the power to call a student to the Bar.

On completion of the Bar Vocational Qualification you need to spend a year in chambers as a 'pupil at the bar'. There is a central application process for pupillages called PACH through which you can apply to up to twelve chambers through a single application. A pupillage is a one-to-one apprentice-style relationship with a junior barrister. For the first six months you are 'non-practising'. During this time you will assist and observe, and also carry out research. After this you are awarded a provisional practising certificate for the following six months you are 'practising' and able to work on your own. You are then awarded a full certificate.

Payment is voluntary for chambers. Currently, there are about 450 paid pupillages (about £3,000 for six months) out of a total on offer of 600.

Finally you need to secure a 'tenancy' (a job in chambers) and your career as a fully qualified barrister begins. You need to undertake Continuing Professional Development (CPD) following your pupillage, including a one-day advocacy course, a two-day advice to counsel course, the New Practitioners' Programme and Compulsory Forensic Accounts Training.

Solicitor/advocate (Scotland) The entry route for solicitors and advocates in Scotland begins with one of a short list of recognised Scottish degrees in law. Non-graduates can complete a three-year pre-diploma training contract with a solicitor and sit examinations set by the Law Society. Alternatively there is an accelerated degree course in law which Honours graduates in other subjects can take.

Solicitor Following your Bachelor of Laws degree (LLB) in Scotland (or equivalent, different from the LLB in England and Wales), there is a new system in place consisting of four stages of training.

1 **The new Postgraduate Diploma in Legal Practice**

After completion of the Scottish LLB degree or Law Society examinations, all intending solicitors are required to take the Diploma in Legal Practice. This lasts seven months. It covers basic skills and knowledge including conveyancing, private client, civil court practice, criminal court practice, company/commercial and public administration. There is also tuition on financial services, accountancy and practice management, and professional ethics.

2 **Post-Diploma training contract**

After the diploma, you serve a two-year training contract with a practising solicitor. This may be in private practice, the Crown Office, local authorities or certain public bodies. The training is monitored by means of logbooks submitted to the Law Society. You can specialise at this stage. After one year you may apply for a qualified practising certificate in order to gain court experience. All training contracts have salaries, based on scales recommended by the Law Society of Scotland.

3 The Professional Competence Course

This three-week course is taken between six months and 18 months into the traineeship but typically at the end of the first year. It covers topics that are more meaningful now that life in the office has been experienced. Subjects include commercial awareness, risk management, complaints and effective legal communication, plus electives of your choice. There is no formal examination.

4 The Test of Professional Competence

This test establishes whether someone is a 'fit and proper' person to be a solicitor. It is taken towards the end of the traineeship. If successful the trainee is entitled to apply for a full practising certificate.

Advocate The Scottish Bar is constituted by the Faculty of Advocates, as part of the College of Justice. The route of entry is very similar to that outlined above for solicitors. In fact, it is recommended that you work as a solicitor for several years before converting to an advocate in order to build up experience and contacts.

Entry begins through completing the degree in Scottish law (as described above). There is no system for non-graduate entry. The next step, shared by would-be solicitors, is to study full-time for a Postgraduate Diploma in Legal Practice. Then follows a period of up to two years in full-time training at a solicitor's office approved by the Faculty. You need also to be formally admitted by the Faculty as an Intrant (trainee advocate).

Next comes about nine months of 'devilling'. This is a period of unpaid practical training with an experienced advocate, your 'devil master'. An examination is set by the Faculty in evidence, pleading, practice and professional conduct. The exam follows an eight-week training period. Then you can start to work as a junior counsel. After seven years at the bar, you can be a devil master; after ten years, a sheriff; and after thirteen years, if you're lucky, a Queen's Counsel.

Solicitor/barrister (Northern Ireland)

The work of barristers and solicitors in Northern Ireland is very similar to that of their counterparts in England and Wales. Differences exist, however, in training procedures.

In order to fulfil entry requirements, law graduates must have studied eight core subjects: constitutional, contract, tort, criminal, land, equity, evidence and European law. To gain knowledge of these subjects, non-law graduates must complete an approved course such as the two-year Bachelor of Legal Science Studies at Queen's University Belfast. Trainee solicitors must register with the Law Society, while trainee barristers need to register with the Inn of Court of Northern Ireland. Maximum numbers of trainees are set to prevent unemployment in the professions. Check current numbers with the Institute of Professional Legal Studies.

Solicitor The Law Society of Northern Ireland has responsibility for the professional training and conduct of solicitors in Northern Ireland. Most solicitors work in private practice; however commercial and industrial organisations also employ solicitors, as do the civil service, State and quasi-State bodies.

There are several routes to becoming a student of the Society and thereby entering the profession. First you need a place at the Institute of Professional Legal Studies, achieved in one of the following ways, so that you can pursue an apprenticeship:

Law degree route You need a qualifying law degree, covering the eight core subjects, and success in the Institute's entrance exam.

Non-law degree route You need a degree in another discipline in addition to a satisfactory level of knowledge of the eight core legal subjects and success in the Institute's entrance exam.

Alternative routes You have reached a satisfactory standard of general education. You are at least 29 and have worked as a clerk or employee of a solicitor for a continuous period of seven years so as to achieve the appropriate level of knowledge and experience of a solicitor's work.

Or, you are at least 30 and have acquired such special qualifications and/or experience as to make you suitable for entry to the Society.

Apprenticeship This two-year sandwich course combines work experience and academic study. For those from the 'alternative routes' it can last four years. There is a small salary. On the two-year programme, the first four months and the last eight months are spent in office training. The middle 12 months are spent at the Institute of Professional Legal Studies. It is the responsibility of the applicants to find themselves an approved solicitor 'master'.

On completion of the training and examinations, a student can apply to be enrolled as a solicitor of the Supreme Court of Judicature in Northern Ireland, and so apply for a practising certificate.

Barrister The Institute of Professional Legal Studies trains barristers as well as solicitors. Once again, to enter the profession you need to gain admittance to the Institute.

Law degree route You need a second class degree in law (covering the core subjects) and a place on the one-year full-time vocational course at the Institute, through successful completion of their entrance examination.

Non-law degree route You need a second class degree in another discipline, a Certificate in Academic Legal Studies and a place at the Institute (as above) through success in the entrance exam.

Pupillage All trainees must complete a 12-month pupillage with a 'master' (an experienced barrister). During the first six months they are not entitled to practise on their own account.

Qualification as a member of the Institute of Legal Executives (ILEX) (England and Wales, no equivalent in Scotland and Northern Ireland) The Institute of Legal Executives is the main route for non-graduates to become solicitors, although many choose to remain simply as qualified legal executives. There are two parts, and a disciplinary code. Part I consists of a broad introduction to the major areas of law. Part II raises the qualification to degree and professional standard and consists of four subjects (three in law, one on practice) reflecting an individual's interests.

People often study for ILEX while working. In order to qualify to begin studying part I you need satisfactory qualifications from your general education. Contact ILEX for more information. Once you have passed the two parts and acquired three years of legal experience you can then enrol on the Legal Practice Course if you wish to become a solicitor. Alternatively, you can gain five years experience in order to qualify fully as a Fellow of ILEX.

Qualification as a legal secretary In England and Wales this is typically a two-year course, which can be split into two one-year courses. The first year of study awards you a certificate, while the second year of study gives you a diploma. Once you obtain the diploma you are a qualified legal secretary. The course covers word-processing, legal text processing, presenting legal reports, book-keeping and also includes an A-level in law. You will need to have attained an appropriate standard in your general education. Sometimes relevant work experience may suffice.

In Scotland the National Certificate in Legal Secretarial Studies lasts one year. The course covers legal text processing and theoretical knowledge of the Scottish legal system, incorporating the Higher in

Administration at Intermediate 2. Two weeks' work experience is also usually included. Typically, entry qualifications for the course exist detailing the qualifications you must possess from your general education.

In Northern Ireland the training for legal secretaries is less specialised. Legal secretaries often just have a general secretarial qualification and possibly some legal experience. There are a few more specialist courses geared to legal secretarial work but these are often not a requirement to finding work.

Work experience It is worth trying to arrange work experience in a legal environment that you are interested in joining. This may be informal work-shadowing that you organise yourself, or a more structured scheme such as those run by some private law firms (especially in the City) and the government legal service during the Easter or summer holidays. Similarly, some barristers' chambers offer mini-pupillages which usually last one week.

4 Funding training

Legal training can be prohibitively expensive and finding funding difficult. Most of the options available only cover the professional qualifications for solicitors and barristers.

General

- **high street bank loan** (various packages for law students who are potentially high earners)
- **Law Society bursaries** for CPE/LPC students of outstanding promise who prove genuine need
- **charities/grant-making trusts** (Skill has a leaflet detailing some that help disabled students)
- **Disabled Students' Allowances** for law students (undergraduates) through relevant funding authority
- **Postgraduates in England/Wales** are also now eligible for DSAs. The LPC is covered but not the CPE. (Bursary and discretionary award schemes in Scotland and Northern Ireland continue as before, and contain DSAs.)

England and Wales

Employer sponsorship Some firms of solicitors pay CPE/LPC fees and maintenance for students they have accepted as trainees.

four

4

Career Development Loan Government loan scheme available from certain banks (Barclays, Clydesdale, Co-op).

Local Education Authority Discretionary grants in cases of need/hardship.

Inns of Court and The Bar Council The Inns of Court provide some awards for the CPE, BVC and pupillages, and the Bar Council offers a small number of interest-free loans.

Northern Ireland

Higher Education Grant Scheme (Bursaries at IPLS) The Professional Course counts as postgraduate study for grant purposes (grant-holders should apply to their local authorities for extensions). Bursaries are available from the Department of Education for Northern Ireland for the Certificate in Professional Legal Studies at the Institute of Professional Legal Studies at Queen's University, Belfast.

Mature Student Grant Scheme Students who are 23 or more on 1 January in the year they begin their course can apply to their local authority for a grant under this scheme.

Law Society Bursary Scheme The Law Society runs a bursary scheme for the CPE/LPC. Students who consider that their own resources or available family resources are inadequate to fund their study can apply.

Scotland

Students Awards Agency for Scotland (SAAS) SAAS gives awards for full-time vocational courses through the Postgraduate Students' Allowances Scheme (PSAS). These are means-tested and cover fees and living costs. PSAS include Disabled Students' Allowances.

The Law Society of Scotland As part of the Scottish Quota for 2000, through SAAS, 300 awards are given to the Law Society of Scotland for applicants who wish to undertake the Diploma in Legal Practice course at a Scottish Institution. There are also scholarships available through the Clark Foundation and the Pritchard Trust.

5 Profiles

My name is Linda Okeke and I have just completed the postgraduate diploma in Legal Practice (LPC). In September I shall be joining Allen & Overy, a large international law firm with main offices in the City of London, as a trainee solicitor.

I became disabled due to a viral infection at the age of eight. I now rely mostly on a wheelchair and crutches for mobility.

For my 'A' Levels, I studied Biology, Chemistry and Physics. **When I was younger, I had wanted to be a solicitor and a doctor! I chose a career in law because I enjoy interaction with people.** I also wanted a career that would offer intellectual challenges, varied career opportunities, and an opportunity to keep learning (glutton for punishment!). I chose a law degree as a route to achieving my goal to become a solicitor.

Before applying, I contacted the universities to discuss their facilities and access issues. I had commitments which meant that I had to study in

London. I must admit that many of the universities I contacted were unhelpful, vague or uncertain about their facilities. Many did not have a disability officer or anyone who could adequately address my concerns.

I chose London Guildhall University because they were professional, interested and supportive of me and my needs. The university had good facilities, an excellent law library, contacts with the City, and was conveniently situated 10 minutes drive from my flat. This came in handy during a few lazy winter mornings!

I started my degree with a positive attitude. I expected a few difficulties and knew I had to be creative, adaptable, flexible, and very patient. For example, the building where I attended most of my classes had two small lifts. Busy students are not concerned with giving priorities to people in wheelchairs! I compensated for this by making sure I allowed plenty of time to get to classes. The library also had top shelves that I couldn't reach. The library staff and other students were always helpful, but I also devised a safe way of getting books from top shelves using my crutches.

In my second year in university, I applied for summer placements with various law firms and obtained a placement at Allen & Overy. I would advise anyone considering a career as a solicitor to apply for a placement. It will help you decide whether a law career is for you, and will also demonstrate your seriousness to prospective employers.

At the end of my second year at university, I applied to various law firms for a training contract. I was apprehensive about applying to the 'top' firms and a few well-meaning people tried to discourage me from 'aiming too high'. An overweight, black female in a wheelchair is hardly the City image! I am definitely not Ally McBeal or LA Law! In fact, a career adviser told me bluntly that I should 'stick to the high street firms'.

I secured interviews at four 'top five' City firms and chose Allen & Overy because of the friendly, young, thoroughly professional image, as well as excellent career and training opportunities. Allen & Overy have been highly supportive of me. **At the end of my law degree, I gained a first class honours degree. The firm rewarded me with a £500 prize which came in handy for a 'poor' student!**

I stayed on at London Guildhall for the LPC because they have a good Law Society rating for the course. They also offered me the course at half the price as a reward for obtaining a first class degree. Allen & Overy paid the rest of my course fees. As preparation for starting work, I have attended various meetings with recruitment staff at Allen & Overy and the Department for Education and Employment. The meetings are aimed at ensuring that their offices are reasonably accessible when I start work. It includes things like building ramps and more disabled toilets.

If you are considering a career in law, do not expect your studies or finding a job to be easy. Be prepared to work extremely hard at both. Good academic results, a determination to succeed, creativity, flexibility and a positive attitude will open doors, which could otherwise remain closed. **Do not allow anyone to discourage or distract you from your goals. Law is highly competitive and image-conscious but times are changing.** Most law firms are now positive about disabled people. I am happy with my chosen career and I am also excited about starting work. **I wish you the best of luck in your future career.**

Arif Khan is a solicitor at the Office of Fair Trading.

I chose law because it was suggested to me as one of four careers that blind people entered (along with physiotherapy, social welfare, and theology).

Studying politics, economics and history at A-level had given me a taste for law. Later I realised that I wanted to use my legal training to solve problems. In particular I wished to help the 'underdog' by protecting the legal rights of people who did not have the legal knowledge to protect themselves. This desire has directed my career path, leading me to choose areas of law such as employment, landlord and tenant, harassment, and my current area of expertise, consumer law.

I trained as a solicitor. I completed 'O' and 'A' levels at two London polytechnics over two years, then read law at Cambridge University. Following this I did a one-year postgraduate degree in International Law and Civil Liberties before studying for the seven papers of the Solicitors' Professional Examination from home in the evenings. I had originally wanted to be a barrister but was advised by another blind person that the nature of the work would present more barriers than that of a solicitor. So I decided to become a solicitor because the emphasis was on desk-based research rather than speed-reading last minute briefs and reflex reactions in court. Sight is more important in an environment where acting on the spot is essential, along with finding papers and relevant pages as soon as possible.

My blindness resulted from a shooting accident when I was fifteen. In 1963 I came to England from Pakistan for treatment but was told there was nothing that could be done. I had to undertake a lengthy rehabilitation process. After this I wanted to study. Worcester School for the Blind rejected me as I had poor English at this time but **I enrolled at two London polytechnics where I had extremely positive experiences and my disability was well supported.** I couldn't read textbooks so, to access material, voluntary organisations made tapes for me, local schoolboys read to me and I made notes in Braille. These three kinds of support continued at Cambridge with the help of students and staff. In addition I was allowed to sit exams in my own room, using a typewriter. Later, when I studied for the Solicitors' Professional Examination at home, friends who were articled clerks made me tapes.

I received good workplace support once I had qualified. The Department of Education and the Office of Fair Trading (previous and current employers) asked about my support needs and obtained equipment. **As a legal director at the Office of Fair Trading, I have a full-time reader (essential with 150 e-mails and many files to read each day)** as well as Braille software and speech function on my computer. Overall there are no real gaps in my support at present but I personally have to be very organised so that my disability is never an excuse.

Various individuals have provided further valuable support. At Cambridge one of my tutors encouraged me towards personal independence as well as independent thinking. **All my tutors were extremely understanding and always ready to resolve problems and answer questions.** Finally, family support is absolutely central, for example, my wife has been reading for me for many, many years.

It was once I put myself on the job market that invisible barriers started to multiply and doors started to close. The Disability Discrimination Act did not exist at this time. I made about 250 unsuccessful applications for articles. It seemed that the legal employment market thought disabled people weren't up to the mark.

On a more practical level, not being able to see and read like sighted people means that I cannot access written information as quickly. I have overcome these different barriers in different ways. When I was unsuccessful in getting articles I became a lecturer at the Inns of Court. In due course I approached my old Cambridge College, where one of the professors very kindly phoned someone who in turn secured me articles. I have overcome the barrier of slower 'reading' by learning to skip and find shortcuts. These skills improve with experience and confidence. In terms of personal qualities, I find that hard work, intelligence, honesty and a good sense of humour form the best policy in combating discrimination. **Determination and commitment are crucial.**

The advice I would give to other disabled people considering a career in law is to be patient, work hard and be determined. **Decide early on what you want to do. Provided you have the ability you will find a way.** Listen too to your elders in the profession, and when you get a job work hard and prove yourself. **There will always be those who discriminate but the majority will change if you demonstrate you are able and willing to do anything.**

Eleanor Williams is a solicitor at Remploy. On my screen saver on my PC, I have the message, 'Nothing wastes time like dodging assassins!' I see it going round and round at odd times during the day. It is a statement that I found hidden in a novel called The Three Hostages by John Buchan. Now, Buchan was a lawyer by profession, but it is for his profuse imagination that he will be remembered.

To qualify as a lawyer had always been my expectation, ever since I first came across John Buchan books in early adolescence. I never envisaged that it might one day be a struggle. However, when at sixteen, I had a massive cerebral haemorrhage leaving me unable to move or speak, my expectations needed realigning.

I could no longer take notes, write exam answers, or get easily from one room to another for lectures and tutorials. This meant reading Jurisprudence at University College, Oxford was tricky. Strangely enough, doing my Law Society final exams at the College of Law in York was easier. I think it was at this stage that I saw first what a difference it makes if you have people around you who are willing you on to succeed. **The staff at York seemed to possess an imagination that realised that my impairments were only physical and did not go to the heart of being a lawyer.**

So now I had the relevant bits of paper that would allow me to practice. But it was now that my physical impairments really 'kicked in'. I needed a Training Contract, signing me up to an apprenticeship and providing me with somewhere I could work for two years before gaining my all important Practising Certificate from the Law Society. I wrote off hundreds of letters and received countless negative responses, not because of my qualifications, but because employers had their offices upstairs, or because they were just plain scared. I was at the end of my tether. My childhood expectations were crumbling.

Then along came Remploy Ltd. As the largest employer of disabled people in the UK, they possessed the requisite imagination to cut through all the difficulties imposed by other employers. I joined their agency, Interwork, and they paid a substantial part of my salary so that I could carry out a Training Contract with Gwent County Council. And when I started to work, I discovered that my impairments did not go to the heart of being a lawyer. I dictated all my letters, I learnt to drive and kept a mobile phone in the dashboard of my car. Thus, I was able to phone the court usher from the car park and he would help me into the court with all my books.

I did not know it at the time, but what I was doing was implementing 'reasonable adjustments'. This phrase became enshrined in the statute books on the passing of the Disability Discrimination Act 1995. **This Act, if properly implemented, can mean that no disabled person should ever find themselves 'short changed' because of their disability.** Really, it is a very imaginative piece of legislation that seeks to enforce a change in public attitude and in social behaviour. And that is something that is not usually so directly addressed by an Act of Parliament. Thanks to the advent of this Act, I could suddenly see the wider picture of disability and the law.

This coincided with my becoming involved with the Law Society. I discovered that there was a Group for Solicitors with Disabilities with nearly 500 members throughout the country. During my year as chair of this group, I was able to discern that disabled people have an affinity for the law. I think this happens for two reasons: first, disabled people tend to have needed to be fairly combative in their attitude to life, and so are attracted to an adversarial profession like the law. Second, disabled people may well have come across the law through their own disability. So, the machinations of law together with its potential benefits might have been observed. Oh, and along the way, **my childhood expectation had, thanks to the imagination of Remploy, of the College of Law and of the Disability Discrimination Act, become a reality.**

I have a sneaking suspicion that disabled people are drawn to the law because disabled people tend to have to be imaginative. Thinking flexibly, planning ahead and solving problems are qualities that make for good lawyers and are essential tools for managing disability. John Buchan, who was dogged by disabling illnesses all his life ended up as Governor General of Canada, perhaps because he could see imaginatively beyond the case he was working on to the bigger picture. The law needs as much imagination as it can get. **The law needs disabled people, people who know that 'Nothing wastes time like dodging assassins!'**

My name is Lee Blakey and I am a 28 year-old barrister practising out of chambers in Preston, Lancashire. I have been partially sighted since the age of one, yet despite this, I have endeavoured to take part in as wide a range of sporting and academic activities as possible. I lost my sight completely at the age of twenty, mid-way through my law degree.

My interest in the legal profession must have started at around the age of 13 or 14. At this time, a friend qualified as a barrister and, in my free time, I would accompany her to court to witness, excuse the pun, the law in action. In addition to this, **while still at school, I obtained a week-long work experience placement at a local firm of solicitors.**

This only served to increase my interest in the profession that I felt sure was the career for me. In 1990 I enrolled on the LLB course at the University of Central Lancashire and, as already indicated, I was partially sighted for the first two years of my degree so I was able to read books, albeit at a slower speed and with the aid of powerful glasses. The loss of the remainder of my sight necessitated the development of a new system of working. I went to the Special Needs Unit at the university and was provided with advice as to how best to continue my studies. Fortunately, while an A-level student, I picked up the valuable skill (so it turned out) of touch typing and this allowed me to work with a computer and accompanying speech synthesiser. I taped my lectures/tutorials and later typed them into my computer so that I was able to have free and easy access to my notes. In addition to this, I made use of the reader service provided by the Special Needs Unit. **The assistance I received throughout my time as an undergraduate was most impressive and the level of assistance received from the Special Needs Unit was most welcome.** To this end, I would encourage you to make the most of this at your university because the assistance will be there.

After graduating in 1994, I moved to London to undertake the year of post-graduate study necessary for all would-be barristers – the Bar Vocational Course. I was at the Inns of Court School of Law (ICSL) from September 1994 until June 1995 and **of over 1,000 people on the course, I finished 165th – an achievement that fills me with a great sense of pride even today.** At the ICSL I adopted a similar working practice to that which worked so well as an undergraduate. I was provided with support from ICSL and Lincoln's Inn, who set aside part of the library for me and my readers.

I was called to the Bar on 11th October 1995 and I undertook my pupillage at 15 Winckley Square, Preston. I have been a tenant there since 2 October 1996. I have a full-time assistant paid for by PACT (Placement, Assessment and Counselling Team, now known as the Disability Service Team). In addition to this, I continue to use a computer with speech synthesiser for the purposes of writing my advices. My practice principally consists of personal injury work, though, in addition to this, I undertake work of a general common law nature. Being blind, I concentrate on a paper work practice (as opposed to court work).

Inevitably, along the way, I have encountered people who did not believe that I could make it this far and people who have expressed great surprise when they found out that I am a barrister. At times, it is necessary to explain to people the system I have in place for working, in order to allay their reservations. However, generally, I have been fortunate throughout my studies, and during practice, to have received a great deal of assistance and support in what I have endeavoured to achieve.

I would recommend a career in the legal profession to any visually impaired person with an

interest in the law. I will not pretend that it is an easy path to follow, and it will involve the inevitability of intense study that the law requires. But with the requisite level of work, and the inspiration that comes from determination, there is no reason why anyone reading this article cannot ultimately succeed in their chosen career. **Good luck!**

Lisa McNulty is a solicitor in Blackburn. It seems a lifetime ago when I was 14, at a Careers Convention. There, I decided to pursue a career in law.

Unfortunately the conventional route into the legal profession was thwarted when I contracted encephalitis, a brain virus, during my A level studies. Due to the virus, I was also diagnosed with epilepsy, which is currently controlled with medication. Well, the best-laid plans often go to waste!

My sixth form principal indicated I would probably not reach the necessary standard in my A level exams, as my virus caused me to sleep a lot – what encouragement! But I could 'go through the motions' and take the exams, and return to do an extra year when my health improved. However, not admitting how ill I really was, I still had unrealistic expectations.

I was obviously devastated when, although I attained 3 A levels very much against the odds, the grades were not good enough to do a law degree. However, the very idea of returning to do an extra year in A level studies was unthinkable – two years had certainly been enough!

I enrolled, after much consultation with tutors, at the University of Central Lancashire, in Preston, for a degree in Education Studies with Health Studies. During my degree, I was aware of my poor A level grades therefore I was concerned that I would not be capable of attaining my degree. So I pulled out the stops, and even used the summer before my final year to start and actually complete my dissertation. **All my efforts paid off when I was the only student on my course to be awarded a first class degree.**

I then started the full-time Common Professional Examination at the University of Central Lancashire. I must admit it was extremely demanding and intensive, though rewarding. My next hurdle was the Legal Practice Course, which I completed at Chester College of Law. **The course passed without incident, other than failing one subject – well, I am only human!**

The remaining obstacle to overcome was my 2-year training contract. I had been aware of the difficulties in securing a contract, and had spent 2 previous summers on work experience at a local firm of solicitors. Thankfully, they offered me a contract. After 2 years I 'graduated' from a trainee solicitor with minimal responsibilities to a qualified solicitor with immense responsibilities.

I had been faced with many obstacles to overcome

in order to reach this stage, so the day on which I qualified was quite emotional. Finally I was able to sit back and relax, or so I thought!

I had been qualified for 19 days when I became quite ill. I was diagnosed with myalgic encephalomyelitis (ME) and ordered to rest. Unfortunately I was unable to do anything other than rest. It is difficult to express on paper my feelings at this stage. At the beginning my consultant said that had I been in my mid-fifties, he would have recommended retirement. As I was in my mid-twenties this was not an option, and I would have to decide my priorities.

I rested for several months, and then gradually started working from home, progressing to part-time work in the office. **I was so determined that my ME would not prevent me from returning to work full time that I stored a camp bed in my office, which I used to recharge my energy at lunchtime.**

The ME was diagnosed two years ago. I have now returned to work on a full-time basis, though still need rest in the evenings and at weekends. My social life is currently on hold; hopefully not for much longer!

I have been promoted to an Associate in the Mental Health Department of my firm, and am a member of the Mental Health Review Tribunal Panel. Initially, I wanted to be a solicitor to help others, and I feel I am able to do this successfully with my personal experience of health issues. **I gain great satisfaction from my career, and am thankful that my determination and perseverance continued – some would even say being stubborn has helped!** Finally, it would not have been possible to reach this stage without the **never-ending support that I have been fortunate to receive from many sources.**

David Gray is a solicitor in private practice in Northern Ireland. At the start of the upper sixth form in 1977 all my plans were for a future in medicine, dentistry or some science-based course. One month later all that was changed by an accident on the rugby pitch. I lay with a broken neck at the start of what was to be almost two years in hospital and a life of using a wheelchair.

The following summer I completed one of my A-level courses, dictating the exam answers as at that stage I was still unable to hold a pen. Matters had improved by the next year when I finished the written papers for 2 further A-levels with a pen firmly strapped to my hand.

By this stage I had opted for law at my local university, The Queen's University of Belfast. My priority was to experience student life, rather than to prepare for any particular profession **but wise family, friends and teachers had recommended that I consider the law as a possible career.** A visit to the law faculty in its Victorian terrace houses had quickly shown it to be totally inaccessible, but the university had bravely committed to providing access to the essential tutorial and lecture rooms if I attained the necessary grades. They were as good as their word and 4 years of study ensued with the valuable additional benefit of some considerate timetabling.

One year through the course I attained my driving licence and the chance to move from home to newly-adapted student accommodation in the university area. Apart from the much-improved social life, the following 3 years of exercise pushing myself around the often circuitous routes about the campus led to better stamina and fitness.

With the degree secured, I then took a 'gap year'. The first six months were **devoted to intensive physiotherapy and training before embarking on my own round-the-world trip through Singapore, Australia, New Zealand, Hawaii and the United States.** After this I resumed my studies again, undertaking the professional courses required to qualify as a solicitor. Again the university undertook the works required to make buildings accessible.

Probably the most difficult stage for anyone seeking to enter the legal profession is to secure a place in an office or chambers. In my case, my parents' solicitor arranged for his court messenger to note any solicitors' offices in the city centre which might be accessible by wheelchair. I then presented myself in turn at various offices to enquire about the possible openings. After several weeks the partner in one of those I visited wrote to say that they would be taking on an apprentice and that I might apply with any others who were interested. **After interviews I was successful and some fifteen years later I am now the senior partner in the firm.**

The law offers the potential for those with disabilities to practise and compete successfully. But it is highly popular and there is a lot of competition for courses and jobs. **Potential employers have a wide choice and it will help if you can point to something on your CV which indicates your ability to cope with difficult situations and if necessary on your own.** Looking back, I suspect that my independent travels may have helped persuade the firm that I joined that it might be worth taking the risk of employing someone with obvious physical difficulties.

If you want a career that offers the opportunity to take on responsibility, to work independently and, with luck, to earn a good living, law may be the right one for you. If you think this could be the case then do try to get some practical experience or time in an office as early as possible.

Shobha Goriah Edgell is a senior court clerk in a magistrates' court in Hertfordshire. I chose a career in law because my parents felt that it was important for their children to have a professional qualification. In due course I obtained a higher national diploma in business studies, an LLB and passed the Bar finals. I chose this route because circumstances enabled me to obtain the HND qualification, which proved a stepping stone to legal training.

I funded myself for the first year of my degree course. I was fortunate to be awarded a scholarship, which helped me enormously. I then married. After university, I took several clerical jobs for a year to help fund Bar school. **My husband was immensely supportive.**

I have faced barriers during the course of my training and work. When I was studying, I was embarrassed and ashamed of my hearing aids. I told no-one of my disability. When sitting my Bar exams, I would switch my aids off as they pick up extraneous noise, which is distracting. After one exam, when the

3 hours were up, I sat up and switched my aids back on. Surprisingly no-one stopped writing for a further half-hour. I found out afterwards that there had been a bomb scare with attendant commotion caused by the emergency services outside. An announcement had been made that examinees would be given an extra half-hour as a result!

I did not tell my pupil master of my disability. I coped well until an occasion when I did not hear my pupil master as he spoke when I was not facing him. He was unhappy that I did not respond. We were both embarrassed when I explained my problem.

I have now learnt to overcome barriers by accepting that I have a problem, telling people how they can help me and taking lip-reading lessons.

The advice I would give to others considering a career in the Bar is **"go for it!"** Tell people of your disability. **Always maintain a positive attitude and explain to those around you how they can help.**

Leigh Rennie is a student at Strathclyde University. For as long as I can remember, my ambition has been to study law and when the results of my Standard Grade exams allowed me to believe I would attain the necessary Highers, I set about looking for law schools with a good academic record. However, this was not the only criterion. The university I would eventually be attending also had to be wheelchair friendly, both in terms of physical accessibility and with regard to their attitude towards me as a wheelchair user.

I chose 3 universities to investigate in greater detail. The practicalities of getting around the first were enormous and much building work would have been required in order to allow me access to many important areas of the campus, for example, the library. The second would also have required some modifications, not least a change in their attitude towards wheelchair users and the issue of accessibility arising from the possibility of a student with mobility concerns attending their establishment. My third visit brought me to Strathclyde. Much of this campus is located on a hill with a very steep gradient, which could potentially have caused me problems with, for example, car-to-wheelchair transfer, and I was therefore put off initially.

However, after being introduced to, and personally shown round the university by their special needs advisor and admissions selector, **I was left in no doubt as to their positive attitude and the fact that they actually wanted me to be there.** During my visit, it was apparent that both members of staff were quite shocked by the many basic facilities which were missing, for example, a wheelchair accessible toilet. This, however, was rectified soon after.

Having decided that Strathclyde would be my university of choice, other alterations were made in order to accommodate my mobility requirements. I was highly impressed by the co-operative, obliging attitude of those involved in arranging such changes. A ramp was installed in the main lecture room which is stepped at either side. This ramp enabled me to sit alongside my colleagues (at least as far as the fourth row from the front) and therefore allowed me to communicate with them naturally, instead of being forced to sit in front of everyone with resultant isolation.

This lecture room in the law faculty is only one of many used throughout the campus for law students, yet it is by far the best in terms of inclusion, a requirement not always apparent to the ambulant in society. Unfortunately, the building in which the law faculty exists does not have parking facilities, but arrangements were made for me to use the designated places in the adjoining building. When the situation has arisen of a subject I was to attend being held elsewhere on the campus, all efforts have been made by the university to relocate any such lecture – almost without exception – successfully. It is, however, unfortunate that other lecture theatres and buildings around the campus are not more easily accessible to wheelchair users, in which case fewer rearrangements would be necessary.

Tutorials are also held in various buildings, and again locations have been changed when possible. As these compulsory group meetings are often held in relatively small rooms, **it has even been known for a tutor to remove shelves from the walls of his office in order to make the area more spacious and allow the accommodation of my chair**, as well as a reasonably sized group, again conferring a positive and practical attitude.

Unfortunately, there are areas which I have found difficulty in, for example the law library, which although accessible in that I am able to enter it, is almost impossible to make proper use of, due to its layout.

As an area where students meet and (quietly) discuss legal issues (as well as social chitchat), I do feel isolated from this. However, **library staff are very helpful in supplying me with necessary reading material on request**, and photocopy anything required, as the facilities do not allow me to do so for myself. Another problem area is the computer room in the law building, which offers internet access. However, the cramped nature of this space bars me from easily benefiting from such a facility.

Furthermore there is the issue of the lack of eating places around the campus which are wheelchair accessible. The nearest to the law faculty requires a convoluted ten minute journey to be undertaken, and when time is short, this again curtails social interaction.

That said, **I have found Strathclyde a university very willing to adapt to my needs as a wheelchair user.** The general attitude is one of wanting to change for the better, to accommodate the requirements of all students who attend it. Although some practical difficulties do remain, **the possibility of a truly accessible and non-discriminatory place of higher learning is in evidence, simply because of the forward-looking approach of the staff and the majority's genuine desire to facilitate improvements.**

6 Useful publications

About Law: An Introduction

Tony Honore (1996). Clarendon Press.

AGCAS Graduate Careers Information 2000

Series on the legal profession. CSU, Crawford House, Precinct Centre, Oxford Road, Manchester M13 9EP. Available from most career services.

The Bridge

A magazine for disabled solicitors produced by Aviva Gully of the Trainee Solicitors' Group (contact details below).

Careers in the Law

Kogan Page, 120 Pentonville Rd, London N1 9JN.

Chambers and Partners Directory

(annually). Chambers and Partners.

Community Legal Service Directory (2000)

Legal Services Commision, 85 Gray's Inn Road, London WC1X 8TX. Tel: 020 7759 0000.

GTI Law Journal – and various supplements

GTI specialist publishers, The Barns, Preston, Crowmarsh, Wallingford, Oxon OX10 6SL. E-mail: gti@gti.co.uk

The Lawyer
A weekly legal rag (www.the-lawyer.co.uk)

Learning the Law, Glanville Williams (1982)
Stevens & Sons. In need of updating but still a useful guide.

The Legal 500, John Pritchard (1999)
Legalease. ISBN: 1870854381
At £100, another one to consult at your library/careers service. Lists the 500 largest law firms in the UK.

Prospects Law, in association with the Law Society and Bar Council
From CSU, Prospects House, Booth Street East, Manchester M13 9EP. Tel: 0161 277 5210.
Guide to training contracts in the legal profession.

Solicitors' and Barristers' National Directory
(annually). The Law Society. Rather expensive at £75.00. Best to find a reference copy.

Working in Law, (1999)
Careers and Occupational Information Centre.
ISBN 0861 107632.

7 Useful contact organisations

The Bar

The Bar Council of Ireland Law Library, PO Box 5939,
Dublin, Ireland. Tel: 00 353 1804 5000.

Central Applications Clearing House (CACH)

The General Council of the Bar (Education and Training
Department), 2/3 Cursitor Street, London EC4A 1NE.
Tel: 020 7440 4000.

Common Professional Examinations Central

Applications Board, PO Box 84, Guildford,
Surrey GU3 1YX. Tel: 01483 451080.

Crown Prosecution Service (CPS)

Recruitment, 50 Ludgate Hill, London EC4M 7EX.
Tel: 020 7796 8000. Internet: www.cps.gov.uk

Faculty of Advocates

Advocates Library, Parliament House,
Edinburgh EH1 1RF. Tel: 0131 226 5071.

The General Council of the Bar

(includes a Disability Committee)
3 Bedford Row, London WC1R 4DB
Tel: 020 7242 0082. Internet: www.barcouncil.org.uk

The General Council of the Bar

Education and Training Department,
2/3 Cursitor Street London EC4A 1NE.
Tel: 020 7440 4000. Internet: www.barcouncil.org.uk/et

Inn of Court of Northern Ireland Bar Library,

Royal Courts of Justice, P.O. Box 414 Chichester
Street, Belfast BT1 3JF. Tel: 028 9056 2349.

The Institute of Barristers' Clerks

4a Essex Court, Temple, London EC4Y 9AJ.
Tel: 020 7353 2699.

The Institute of Professional Legal Studies

The Queen's University of Belfast,
10 Lennoxvale, Belfast BT9 5BY
Tel: 028 9033 5567. E-mail: p.rodway@qub.ac.uk
Internet: www.qub.ac.uk/ipls

Bar Association for Local Government and the Public Service

c/o Mirza Ahmed, Bolton Metropolitan Borough
Council, Town Hall, Bolton BL1 1RU.
Tel: 01204 522311/333333
Internet: www.balgps.freeserve.co.uk

Common Professional Examinations Central Applications Board

PO Box 84, Guildford, Surrey GU3 1YX.

Tel: 01483 451080.

Group for Solicitors with Disabilities

c/o Judith McDermott, The Law Society,

114 Chancery Lane, London WC2A 1PL.

Tel: 020 7320 5793.

Institute of Professional Legal Studies (as above)

The Law Society

113 Chancery Lane, London WC2A 1PL.

Tel: 020 7242 1222.

Student Enquiry Line: 0870 606 2555.

Internet: www.lawsociety.org.uk

The Law Society of Northern Ireland

Law Society House, 98 Victoria Street,

Belfast BT1 3JZ. Tel: 028 9023 1614.

The Law Society of Scotland

26 Drumsheugh Gardens, Edinburgh EH3 7YR.

Tel: 0131 226 7411. Internet: www.lawscot.org.uk

Legal Practice Course Applications Board

PO Box 84, Guildford, Surrey GU3 1YX.
Tel: 01483 301282.

Trainee Solicitors' Group

Aviva Gully, The Law Society, 114 Chancery Lane,
London WC2A 1PL.
Tel: 020 7320 5794. Internet: www.tsg.org.uk

Young Solicitors' Group

c/o Judith McDermott, The Law Society,
114 Chancery Lane, London WC2A 1PL.

Additional contacts

Department of Education for Northern Ireland (DENI)

Rathgael House, Balloo Road, Bangor,
County Down BT19 7PR. Tel: 028 9127 9279.
Internet: www.deni.gov.uk

Disability Law Service

Ground floor, 39-45 Cavell Street, London E1 2BP.
Tel: 020 7791 3131. Minicom: 020 7791 2626.
E-mail:advice@dls.org.uk

Government Legal Service Recruitment Team
Queen Anne's Chambers,
28 Broadway, London SW1H 9JS.
Tel: 020 7210 3304.
Internet: doctorjob.co.uk/employers/gls.htm

Institute of Legal Executives (ILEX)
Kempston Manor, Kempston, Bedford MK42 7AB.
Tel: 01234 845718 / 841000. Internet: www.ilex.org.uk

The Law Centres Federation
Duchess House, 18-19 Warren Street,
London W1P 5DB. Tel: 020 7387 8570.

The Law Commission
Conquest House, 37/38 John Street, Theobalds Road,
London WC1N 2BQ. Tel: 020 7453 1210.

Legable (part of Workable, work-placement
charity for disabled graduates)
67-71 Goswell Road, London EC1V 7EP.
Tel: 0207 608 3161. E-mail: joksweeney@aol.com

Legal Action Group
242 Pentonville Road, London N1 9UN.
Tel: 020 7833 2931. Internet: www.lag.org.uk

RNIB (Royal National Institute for the Blind)
Includes a Law library
224 Great Portland Street, London W1N 6AA.
Tel: 0345 023 153. E-mail: helpline@rnib.org.uk

Students Awards Agency for Scotland
Gyleview House, 3 Redheughs Rigg
Edinburgh EH12 9HH. Tel: 0131 476 8212.
Internet: www.student-support-saas.gov.uk